# The CLOSET POET'S Collection

MY LIFE IN VERSE 1969 to 2014

The Closet Poet's Collection - My Life in Verse 1969 to 2014
© Wayne Pendleton 2015

All rights reserved. No part of this publication may be reproduced, stored in a retrieval system, or transmitted in any form or by any means, electronic, mechanical, photocopying, recording or otherwise, without the prior written permission of the author.

National Library of Australia Cataloguing-in-Publication entry (pbk)

| | |
|---|---|
| Author: | Pendleton, Wayne, author. |
| Title: | The Closet Poet's Collection - My Life in Verse 1969 to 2014 / Wayne Pendleton. |
| ISBN: | 9780994236302 (paperback) |
| Subjects: | Pendleton, Wayne--Poetry. Biographical poetry. Prose poems. |
| Dewey Number: | A821.4 |

Published by Wayne Pendleton and InHouse Publishing
www.inhousepublishing.com.au

## Introduction

This closet writing of poetry all started in Winnipeg, Canada, in 1969. Employed as a socio-economic researcher, one of the key job requirements was to write up reports on my findings. My lack of creativity was reflected in my rather bland reports. So in an attempt to rectify this situation I enrolled in a Creative Writing course. The instructor encouraged us to start with something with which we were familiar. My first attempt was a short story about a rebellious high school student of mine in my previous life as a teacher in rural Alberta. As the classes proceeded through various types of creative writing, poetry caught my fancy even though I had never enjoyed reading it previously. Writing it was different. It allowed expression in a new and exciting way.

Since the most inspirational person in my life was my mother, now deceased, I dedicate this collection to her memory. Love you, Mom!

The sequence of poems has some significance, opening with a character sketch of my mother, then tracing my search for a place in life through travel and women, and ending with poems about genuine love. Enjoy the journey!

# Table of Contents

The Widow..................................................................7
Upon a Pedestal........................................................10
Suicide of Love.........................................................11
Doubt?......................................................................13
Fine Line Between...................................................14
A Forlorn Lover's Lament........................................15
Undecided Love.......................................................17
Lover's Choice.........................................................18
Love Growth............................................................19
Mile High Attraction...............................................20
Last Words...............................................................22
Flame of Misfortune................................................24
Anaesthesia – Part One............................................26
Engagement of Friends............................................27
Twenty Years On.....................................................28
You Can't Change That!..........................................31

Story Clouds..................................................................34
Man's Estate..................................................................35
Long Beach - Otago.....................................................37
Images of Noosaville....................................................38
Travel Modes – Europe 2013.............................................40
Travel Modes – England and United Arab Emirates 2013...43
Rush Hour on the Danube – 7am 26 August 2013...........47
Another Lock Another Hour – 7am 31 August 2013......48
Would I Care So?..........................................................50
When 2 = 1....................................................................51
Forty-Eight Ways to Love Your Wife!..........................52
Come to Me Darling......................................................54
Ode to Thirty-Five Married Years................................56
Christmas 1999..............................................................57
Darling Dalene...............................................................59
Our Mother Helen Part One – First Fifty Years.....................60
Our Mother Helen Part Two – Last Forty Years.................63
My Friend, Shorty (upcoming autobiography excerpt).........69

Wayne Pendleton

## *The Widow*

Death as a part of living
Fate makes her tired of giving
Love sincere to chosen mate
                        Second World War overseas
                        Wounds in action Lord decrees
                        End of line for first to rate
Children were two: what to do!
Discipline needed: would she do?
Two years produced second mate
                        A farmer he good as best
                        Time, energy he'd invest
                        The staff of life to create
Tilling the soil food for Gail
Lightning did strike sorry tale
Get him breathing, No! Too late!
                        Expecting her fourth: what to do!
                        Education comes: 'cision due
                        Whether to seek a third mate
Attention required solely give
Surviving children three do live
When on own will be too late?
                        Death as a part of living
                        Fate makes her tired of giving
                        Love sincere to chosen mate

*Attraction*

*Infatuation*

*Emotions*

*Desire*

## *Upon a Pedestal*

Deserving or not
My dear I'm fraught
With want to worship you

Upon a ped'stal
I do install
For all to look and view

With talent galore
Writing and art shore
And core reality – you

Fulfilment cometh
Your life shareth
Much with many – not few

Complications are
A fear – so far
Take care! Love may ensue

# *Suicide of Love*

Invasion of thought
*Constantly*

Daydreaming is naught
*But of you*

Sleep always induced
*Memories*

My actions controlled
*Daily done*

Awakened early
*'magined touch*

Meaning is added
*More living*

What right to control
*My being*

Presence from afar
*Yet so near*

Within me exists
*Love sincere*

But what of children
*Yours and his*

Banish thoughts of you
*Possible?*

Not on this earth dear
*Life would stop*

Compromise may come
*If willing*

Family – all things
*Meaning more*

Than total concern
*Of lov'd one*

Solution non-exist
*Our problem*

Yet many others' too
*Not be first*

Selfishness exists
*Simple – end!*

Wayne Pendleton

## *Doubt?*

How could I doubt her?
I'll never know
She's doing her best
Her love to show

Perhaps I doubt me
Heaven forbid!
A goal I now have
Despair is rid

Self-confidence now
Was built anew
Through total concern
From her love true

Why did I love her?
Could it have been?
Our desires and needs
From above seen

Opening for both
The chance to share
Our lives together
Oh! How we care

How could I doubt her?
*Couldn't, it's plain*
Perhaps I doubt me
Never again

## *Fine Line Between*

*fine line between*

loving/hating

trial of passion

vial of poison

soft tender caresses

blows of frustration

deep-seated meaning

no meaning

cruel indifference

children for sharing

forced pregnancy

love all-consuming

hatred devouring

*fine line between*

Wayne Pendleton

# *A Forlorn Lover's Lament*

All I ask for is a line

To say you've not forgotten

Or, if you have

Then a word

To end this misery

That wells within me

Thinking of those good times

*Lost forever*

                As I wallow

                In my own self pity

At being rejected

Am I but a mixed-up fool

To dream of tomorrow

Never to be

Love turned off

Like a water tap

Sealed to eternity

*Never again to flow*

                Why me? I ask

                Why not? you say


Except you say nothing, no

Not even

"Forget you ever knew me"

Anything beats nothing

Communicate

Fornicate

Convey your message

*In a format that suits*

                A final no

                Or a final yes

Degenerate

That I may be

Regrets overwhelm

I deserve better

Than nothing

                Forever

Wayne Pendleton

## *Undecided Love*

Undecided love
Runs strong
Blows cold
On again, off again

                Frustrated
                Indecision
                Marriage flounders
                On suspicion

Pride refuses
Total commitment
Morals refuse
Reassessment

                Opposite views on
                Love possessed
                Future will build
                On sins confessed

Undecided love
Runs strong
Blows cold
On again
Off again

## *Lovers' Choice*

Skin on skin
Night begins
Passion possessed
Dangers ignored

Adulterous
Longing
Overcomes
Logic

Enjoyment
Satisfaction
Outweighs
Doubts

Remember
Careful
----- Ooh!
Feels good

He's married
I'm single
Shouldn't
----- done

Wayne Pendleton

# *Love Growth*

*First*

She was someone to
-       share my bed
-       cook my meals
-       iron my shirts
-       keep my house

*Then*

We
-       climbed glaciers
-       swam rivers
-       combed beaches
-       picked flowers
-       collected fruit
-       caressed cats
-       visited friends
-       viewed harbours
-       walked paths
-       toured cities
-       dined restaurants
-       cruised sounds

Together

*Now*

I love her

## *Mile High Attraction*

Mile high means
Denver
*But we weren't there*
Mile high club means
Sex in the sky
*But we weren't there*
Mile high attraction means
Getting to know someone
*Yes we were there*

        The clouds, not angel ones
        But tall elegant towers
        *Billowing out en masse*
        Honolulu at night
        Airport wander
        *Missed chance to dance*
        Cuddling the night away
        Wondering if
        *The club's a chance*

                Seventeen hours just us
                Seen as though a couple
                *By stewardess*
                Vancouver the end
                Of mile high tryst
                *Maybe not says he*
                Possible night's delay
                They wonder together
                *Maybe not says she*

Banff for birthday  
Event intervenes  
*Alas! This cannot be*  
To Australia return  
He earlier than she  
*To meet can it be*  
Tuesday class – early end  
Coffee at the point – neat  
*Then metres high not mile*  

        Phone calls and emails yes  
        Plans to meet, but only one  
        *She's crook for just a while*  
        She'll bounce back no doubt  
        Return of gleam to bright eyes  
        *Sickness not a distraction*  
        What's in the future for these two  
        Unknown, but soon may give up  
        *On their mile high attraction*

## *Last Words*

Today

I throw myself to the sharks
I'll just give it away
This wasted life
Thirty-four years
Accomplishments – nil

Escape

Into death via the sea
Hurry yonder fin
End it all now
Stop all further
Unhappiness – please

Others

Have suffered much from me
In my search for love,
Life, happiness
Finding nothing
But loneliness – sad

But truth

It's conveyed by my latest
Who communicates naught
But petty words
Which illustrate
Such emptiness - end

# Events

# and

# Experiences

# *Flame of Misfortune*

Detour ahead

Alas! No brakes

What now, you say

A look we'll take

                Back wheels on fire

                Quick! Out with the kids

                Throw dirt on the fire

                Bang! Down the car skids

Move far away

Gas tank to explode

Keep the kids back

Try to unload

                Car top carrier

                Weighs a ton

                What luck! At least

                We hurt no one

Advised to drive

Till rubber falls free

Behind the wheel

No gears with to flee

Wayne Pendleton

Insides aflame

Side window caves in

Burns dishes, toys

What was our big sin?

                              Gas boils and burns

                              More rubber ignites

                              What do we do?

                              Not a town in sight

We stand in dismay

That car was a dear

Fire has caused us

To shed a tear

                              Battery explodes

                              What a black mess!

                              Journey on, we're

                              Worth a lot less

## *Anaesthesia – Part One*

Coppery flames searing ever upward

Reaching for the top --- of what?

Shrouds of black --- could be smouldering smoke

Suffocating downward

Copper meets black in constantly changing

Jagged diagonal line forming

*Chain of lightning*


The sound of a million cymbals clashing

Tumultuously --- without rhythm

Amplification of stomach growling, heart pounding

Blood rushing

Murmur of doctor making small talk amplifies,

distorts

Becomes soprano singing,

Then nothing – can't see, hear, feel, taste, imagine

--- *nothing*

## *Engagement of Friends*

*Togetherness is the game*
*Forever is its duration*
You both lose or
You both win

*Tonight is a prelude*
Opening innings commence
On the day you wed
Each action taken
Affects two now

*Never take for granted*
Thoughtful deeds, loving caresses
Pave a smooth pathway
Through life's trials
Temptations and tribulations

Care for each other
Share true happiness
*Togetherness is the game*
*Forever is its duration*

## *Twenty Years On*

Has it really been twenty years?
From Jindalee to Wahroonga
With Mark just a baby
And Scott rather young

*Then*

The trailer pushed us home
To Holland Park via Moorooka
Nursery Road and Yuletide Street
Joachim Street next to the Lewises

Home sweet home
For five long years
You hated the stove
And loved the space

Our daughter brought such joy
She showed contentment from the start
We prospered and I grew restless
Desirous of ministry

*Then*

We traversed the Pacific
To L.A. smog and hustle
The fellowship was sweet
The ministry fulfilling

Finances let us down
We returned to uncertainty
TAFE was my fate
Stats was yours

But not for long, Scan
Became your office home
We prospered and I grew restless
Desirous of ministry

*Then*

The WORD in every tongue
Was our call and desire
But past sins decreed
It should not be

Intensified our Christian chores
Me with adults, you with bubs
Family continued to grow and fight
Scott added Natalie to our delight

Old friends come and go
Churches and/or heaven bound
We prospered and I grew restless
Desirous of TAFE escape

Both your parents gone
Your "worth" improved
Temporarily, as
Pool was built

I lost your "worth"
Carter first, then to shade
Through all this
There was the BOOK

Consuming time
And quality of life
We didn't prosper and I more restless
More desirous TAFE escape

*Then*

The hours doubled, but
Enjoyment followed
We sure did miss our Mark
But drew closer to Jane

The finished book
Relieved some pressure
Sharing your job
Gave you a buzz

Visitors from Japan
Replaced the pressure
We prospered and I became restless
Effort in marriage began afresh

*Then*

Who knows?
Another twenty years?
All our children
With children of their own

Grandchildren in Asia
Others in the Pacific
Mine in Canada
Yours in Australia

We retire to the North Pole
Or is it the South?
We prosper, I write, you dote
Companions forever, Amen!

Wayne Pendleton

# *You Can't Change That!*

Half a century  
Reached today  
It is not cricket  
Thank goodness, you say  

                                    Half a lifetime for some  
                             Your Nan and the Queen's mom  
                                   Two thousand and fifty  
                                  Will arrive most quickly  

Enough of the future  
Remember the past  
At the Diamond Drill  
Where I found you at last  

                                    You welcomed me soon  
                                    To your Moorooka home  
                                        Family ready made  
                                    I, no longer to roam  

Into our life came  
This bright little chap  
Conversation at two  
No closing his yap  

                                    Let's not forget the joy  
                                    Mark brought to our life  
                                    Enough for a century  
                                    Ignore all the strife

And then came the princess
With strong will and all
Through love and caring
She'll not likely fall

                        Next came the grandson
                        To bring cheer and a smile
                            To brighten our days
                            And naturally beguile

Our travels were many
To Canada most often
You lifted the spirits
Of my friends and kin

                        Infectious good humour
                            That influences others
                        To home group members
                          A special extra mother

Fifty you really are
You can't change that
Be thankful for all
God set in your path

Wayne Pendleton

*Scenery*

*Nature*

*Travel*

## *Story Clouds*

*Angels*
> flocking to the wind
> feathers or down
> in clusters flowing

*The bear*
> paws stretched up azure
> points north to homeland
> polar dreaming

*He's changed*
> could it be a deer?
> legs elongated
> gently playing

*Puppy*
> now with such smug face
> tail wagging gaily
> friendly greeting

*A branch*
> now appears above
> he grasps and becomes
> monkey swinging

*A man*
> you say – club in hand?
> evolution, you're
> really saying

Wayne Pendleton

# *Man's Estate*

I'm a happy wandering gypsy
Travelling this vast new land
Seeing without understanding
Hearing yet no comprehension
Smelling still not savouring
Wondering but no answers

From the barren arctic tundra
To the Mississippi delta
Spending as though wealthy
Fasting as though a pauper
Cities are different yet the same
Slums, riches, friendly, miserable

Beauty lost, raped by human hand
What is left of the real world?
The country has lost it all – look around
The pungent swampland of the south
The clear dry heat of the desert
The green freshness of the foothills

Mountain streams flow – cold and clear
Across crop yielding prairie fields
Forming lakes teeming with trout
On through mineral under laid forests
To saltwater bays of cod
Is man destroying his own estate?

God-given right to develop
Yet we greedily destroy
Not caring what we leave behind
Let's start using without taking
Producing needs without plundering
Passing on earth beautiful as received

I'm a happy wandering gypsy
Travelling this vast new land
Now seeing with understanding
Through hearing by comprehension
Still smelling, now savouring
Wondering – are these answers?

Wayne Pendleton

# *Long Beach - Otago*

Awe-inspiring cliff face juts high
'bove rolling dunes clad in grass, lupin
Bared to white caps breaking on mat

Standing-start-up trail bike rider
Shatters relaxing peaceful sounds
Twittering birds, beating surf

Hovering gull surveying beach
Horizon search reveals white sail
Sky overcast determined sun

Glittering sand granulated
As sugar fine, shimmering plumes
Of grass protrude blooms floral maize

Domestic cat exploring on
Sniffs entrance now to rabbit lair
Owners watchful lest lost to view

*Engrossed are they in own pursuits*
*Impressions of surrounding scene*
*Artist in sketch, poet in verse*

## *Images of Noosaville*

The light shimmers on river surface
Paints foreground to holiday retreat
The gentle glide of pelican
Barely breaks shimmering surface
*Silence broken by motorboat*

Casual stroll of passers-by
Desire fitness or tension relief
Boats at anchor sway to and fro
Masts extended skyward gleaming
*Silence broken by cockatoo*

Tour boat loading for everglade tour
Children floating on boogie board
Gliding pelican checks me out
Noosa Heads silhouette to nor'east
*Silence broken by street traffic*

Pelican airborne to jetty perch
Orange buoys warn of low water
Golden lab on lead with jogger
Black and white bird checks me out
*Silence broken by bird songs gentle*

Boathouse deep in river's edge
Tinnie follows boathouse in
Deep trough waves slap sandy shoreline
Mixed flora surrounds picnic spot
*Silence surrounded by cicada hum*

Wayne Pendleton

Distant resorts reflect sun's rays
Speedboat leaves showering wake
Smoke-stained brick barbecue awaits
Golden lab returns with human mate
*Silence broken by car radio volume*

Tour boat loaded now departs
For everglades and Harry's Hut
Vacant units suggest too early
For holidaying city slickers
*Silence broken by guide's speaker*

Girl in straw hat on playground swing
Adolescent tries net fishing
Walkers increase in frequency
Along the tree-stumped river bank
*Silence broken as children call*

Anchor ropes tighten from tidal strength
Sparrow flies boat to shore return
Actions increase on river playground
Sand crabs appear and disappear
*Silence broken by motorboat*

Kayaker paddles quickly past
Yellow butterfly flutters by
Black and white bird checks me again
Water skiers cruise the width
*Silence broken bird territorial*

*I'll leave you to it mate! It's yours!*

## *Travel Modes - Europe 2013*

We had opportunities
But didn't take them
Horse drawn carriages
I'm talking about
Every other mode imaginable
Became our mode of transportation

It started simple enough
Our own car to the airport
Then an Emirates plane
Via Singapore to Dubai
Followed by taxi from
Terminal Three to Novotel

Then walking to nearest
Air-conditioned shopping mall
Before first night's sleep
In unique en suite
With separate cubicles
For toilet, shower, and vanity

Air travel again to Prague
And atrium-centred Hilton
Three days there involved
Lots of walking – Charles Bridge and more
Plus coach day tour to
Oddity of bone church

The Czech countryside was scenic
As were the city buildings
Unique architecture at its best

Plus opulence in full array
Such as the cathedral of St Vitus
Within the palatial grounds of Prague castle

A highway coach was next
On a day's journey to
The jewel of the Danube
Budapest where we
Switched modes again
To cruise ship Viking Aegir

This river ship became home base
For thirteen days mainly for
Sleeping and eating, but also
Making friends over cocktails and meals
Our ventures off-board were treats, thanks to
Intimate knowledge of local guides

The combined modes of walking
And buses filled our time off-ship
On-ship we sailed smoothly past
Castles, fortresses, towns with
Churches, cathedrals, bridges,
Industrial plants, plus more

Is a lock a mode of transport?
Perhaps if you include
Highways, rivers, subways
Railroads, footpaths, lifts
Escalators, moving walkways,
Walking trails and stairways

When the cruise ended
It was taxi cab once more
In Amsterdam much walking led
To Anne Frank's house, then
Canal cruised for city views
No time for Rijk Museum, worst luck!

The fast train to Paris was next
Speed limited photos taken
Plus reverse seating didn't help
Almost missed it due to
Directions from kind taxi driver
And my independent streak

Our location in Paris was superb
Walking became mode everywhere
Although the hop-on hop-off bus
Proved somewhat useful
To get us to the Louvre and
Out of the torrential rain

Gave climb of Eiffel tower a miss
But photos reveal we were near
The Arc de Triomphe proved a treat
Then we walked the full length of
The Champs de Elysee's many shops
With photo shoots along the way

When we arrived in Paris
The taxi ride was short
When we left, it was long and eventful
How do Parisians cope without
Traffic lanes and indicators? Answer:
They just push their way through!

Wayne Pendleton

# *Travel Modes -*
# *England and United Arab Emirates*
# *2013*

A short hop via Flybe jet
Paris to Manchester met by Mark
He and Dan rented a car
To show us around their home city, Sheffield
This they did along with dog Janet
All five of us loved the Moors

Of the Peaks District National Park
As well as the unique towns within
Including Bakewell and Tideswell
Then we and Mark wandered the grounds of
Chatsworth House while Janet and Dan
Foraged for mushrooms and berries

After a three-day visit
We were dropped at the train station
Sheffield to St Pancras International
In the centre of London
Short and scenic the trip
This time facing forward!

The toughest part of the trip to this point was
Picking up our London Pass
At Leicester Square with trailing luggage
Once that chore was complete, mode became
The Underground to the hotel
And for three solid days

The tube was quick, efficient and
Easy to more or less master
To the Victoria and Albert museum first
Then the next morning the walking tour from
Westminster station the long way around
To the afternoon Buckingham Palace tour

There is one word that best describes the Palace
Opulence in unlimited measure
Well, maybe grandeur as well
I tried to imagine the grandchildren
Playing amongst the crown jewels
Coronation robes and thrones

It didn't quite fit!
This had to be seen to be believed
Security as tight as an international flight
Probably more so, with staff positioned
Every few feet inside plus
Only metres apart in the Royal Gardens

Early next morning by tube
To Westminster pier to spend
A few hours on the Thames
Passing many famous icons
London Eye and Big Ben clock tower
London Bridge and the Gherkin

Next we explored the Tower grounds
Torture chambers, armour from every era
Military history museum
Climbed the white tower
But most importantly walked past
The real thing: The Crown Jewels

The tube faithfully returned us to our hotel
Plus took us next morning to St Pancras
Here we caught the train to Gatwick
Where we thought our hire car would be
It was at Crawley instead, so
Some hassles but latest travel mode began

A hire car to cover
The entire southern coastline
Then touching on Wales
Through the Lakes District
To Scotland – Edinburgh at least
Back through Yorkshire Dales to Sheffield

Alas, that plan got scuttled
The southern coast took three
Plus a bit days instead of two
The Cotswolds – more than two days behind
Plan B in place we headed east
Around Birmingham to Stamford

The 23rd became ancestor day
The grave of Sue's Uncle Jim in
Coningsby war cemetery
Wayne's tenth great grandfather
William Brewster's birthplace, part of
The Pilgrim Trail – Scrooby

Full circle Sheffield for last night
Only Mark and Janet at home
Dan cooking on Thames river boat
Scenic route Manchester airport
Fly A380 Dubai bound
For maximum use two day Big Bus Tour

From Deira hotel to Burj al Arab
Then Souk Madinat Jumeirah
Unique shops and eateries
Next stop Mall of the Emirates
Occupied by skiers and penguins
Spectators crowd windows for closer look

The Dubai Mall attractions next
All kinds of water creatures swim
In oversized aquarium
Three storey high Olympic pool length
Skating rink of similar length
Enough of modes we're heading home

Wayne Pendleton

# *Rush Hour on the Danube - 7am 26 August 2013*

Up river it happens
Upon the blue Danube
Blue, really murky green
In early morning haze
The Viking staff member
Raises a flag rear ship
Crossing Slovak border
Ten long hours from the *Pearl*

First sign water traffic
Two boats do mid-stream hug
Tug and what? Do not know
Downstream bound Budapest
Ship's wash attacks left bank
Sound smacks like surfing wave
On right appears a ship
Friend or foe will now show

Flashing light above deck
Warns our captain: avoid
*Bolero* is its name
Company not displayed
Our name displayed: *Aegir*
Viking folklore fame
Life saving orange ring
*Ariana* passes

## *Another Lock Another Hour - 7am 31 August 2013*

Ducks depart the canal
As the Aegir gains speed
Which one of sixty-six
Unknown – many through night

We pass under a bridge
Captain's wheelhouse lowered
Along with canopy
Sun deck now off-limits

Spectacular sunrise
Two mornings in a row
Fishermen on east bank
They wait and stare at us

Rapids flow in from right
From rear the sun parts clouds
Stone channel forms rain drain
Stone edge thwarts erosion

Nature relax process
Aided by soft music
As the Aegir glides west
Through historical sites

Interrupted by locks
Many through Germany
Danube, canal, and Main
Main, canal, and Rhine

Nuremberg for today
Then Bamberg and Cologne
More towns, then Amsterdam
**Final destination**

*True Love -*

*Marital*

*Familial*

*Maternal*

## *Would I Care So?*

Were it not love
Would I care so?
Controlled desire
My love still show

>Complex, simple
>Which of two is?
>Thoughts seldom change
>Domestic bliss

Talk unending
Of the future
Love so precious
But are we sure

>Daydreams are filled
>With tomorrow
>Pray ends not in
>Tragic sorrow

Alone, but to-
gether at night
Imag'nation
Doth hold her tight

>Must our marriage
>Cometh so slow?
>Were it not love
>Would I care so?

## *When 2 = 1*

Two become one

        Something special

        Other person first

        **Harmony**

        Selfishness out

**Selflessness in**

        Is this easy?

        Well, not really

        How is it achieved?

        With constant **effort**

        Result of that effort

        **A blessed life together.**

## *Forty-Eight Ways to Love Your Wife!*

How do I love you?
Let me count the ways
At least forty-eight of them
Are coming today

      Spiritually united
      Physically aroused
      Emotionally dependent
      Intellectually complemented

We live our lives daily
With a little bit of drift
As the empty nest approaches
We wonder what's next

      Travel is a common interest
      Where to, who knows
      Each with personal space
      Towards a common goal

Words fail to reflect
How special you are
Hugs and kisses tell
My inner feelings – care

    Ever faithful, ever loyal
    My life is complete
    Bonded to God together
    We meet at His feet

Awesome it truly is
That God knew my needs
And picked you for my partner
From away across the seas

    If I'd picked you myself
    Nothing would I change
    Well, maybe just a little!
    Just joking my dear!

Eros is superb
Filial a treat
Agape a struggle
For this aging beast

    Thanks for the tolerance
    Patience and joy
    You bring with forgiveness
    To this frivolous "boy"

# *Come to Me Darling*

## *A Love Song*

I've travelled around
        From town to town
Sometimes I'm up
        More often I'm down
Searching the world
        For that one true love
Now that I've found you
        Thank heavens above

*Chorus:*

*Come to me darling*
        *I'm waiting for you*
*Come to me darling*
        *I'll always be true*
*I'll never wander*
        *Or stray from your side*
*Come to me darling*
        *With me you'll abide*

Others I have loved
        Were just make believe
Compared to the feeling
        For you that's conceived
No other could envelop
        My every thought
My search for love is ended
        I've found what I sought

*Chorus*

Join with me darling
        I beg and I plead
Our future together
        We'll plan now indeed
Without you I'm worthless
        Of that there's no doubt
Our marriage is certain
        That's what love's all about

*Chorus*

## *Ode to Thirty-Five Married Years*

Goodness gracious, how can it be?
Thirty-five as two, you and me
Those years have flown
They were our own
Enjoyed
Treasured
Cherished
Valued

Trials
And hurts
Overcome
By love
Endowed
As God
Cements the bond

How many more?
Who can guess?
Lord comes before
Or death makes less
Matters not what's in store
Love now and ignore the rest

Wayne Pendleton

# *Christmas 1999*

*To my wife and lover*

Ups and downs
High and low
Throughout it all
I love you so

The shock of Mark
Nearly, not quite
Put out the spark
But not the light

How did we cope?
Lord only knows
Our spirits touched
By home group close

Japan was special
Miyajima Island
Unique cuisine
At stop unplanned

Romantic Sydney
Enthralled by harbour
Beach at Manly
The Heads and more

Our daughter gone
Adventure true
Canada tour
Brought tears from you

Her voice rang joy
To parents' hearts
They wait return
From foreign parts

Happiness within
A special treat
When at airport
We went to meet

Remember ups
Forget the low
I love you more
Than you could know

Wayne Pendleton

## *Darling Dalene*

Petite and trim

Nimble and swift

Blonde hair turns dark

Brushed smooth as silk


Brown eyes catch mine

Twinkle and grin

She hugs my neck

So gently now


I whisker rub

Her dimpled chin

She giggles, laughs

And squirms a bit


*Daddy loves you*

*Darling Dalene*

# *Our Mother Helen*
# *Part One – First Fifty Years*

So many struggles in her long life
Giving herself to three as a wife
Watching her die on her bed brought strife
Our hope that now she has renewed life

Everything, they say, comes in threes
Widowed by two plus one makes three
Children four less one leaves three
Let it be dear Lord! Let it be!

It starts nineteen seventeen
Born to Ethel and Martin
Sister for Merle and Melvin
Married thirty-six to Merlyn

Lloyd was first then came Wayne
First son suffered much pain
To save from burns proved vain
Forty-six passed away

Widowed twice before
Merlyn dead four-four
Volunteer for war
Italy the score

Wayne Pendleton

Two years of grief
Then came relief
Courtship was brief
Married four-six

Love was strong
Not for long
Struck lightning
Must be wrong

Widow
What now?
Don't know
Must go

On
To
Raise
Children

Mom pale
Weep wail
Born Gail
Shan't fail

Gordon's one
Still to come
Bring her home
Fifty-one

Early she came
Laura her name
Nothing the same
Mom felt so lame

Children are now three
No-one to help agree
Where we should be
Can't live in a tree!

More of tired – all in
Irma to start life again
Grandparents took us in
How to start life again

Soon we moved to rented house
Clean but still 'casional mouse
At least no need to delouse
Lonely though without a spouse

An established house – able to buy
Lonely still – one very long sigh
One flirtation with guy named Sy
Still many years just the kids and I

Children have all grown and left the nest
Hard to say who will turn out best
Laura, Gail, Wayne – they have all met the test
Whatever happens, I'm truly blessed

Wayne Pendleton

# *Our Mother Helen*
# *Part Two - Last Forty Years*

Keep
On
With
Life

Lonely
For me
Can't see
Me free

No love new
Has to do
Perhaps true
Just make do

Parents pass on
Children move on
Grandkids come on
Mother stays on

Twenty years it took
To receive loving look
According to book
Or am I mistook

Third husband is Alwyn
Nineteen seventy-one
New life once more begins
Bad at first, Alwyn's sin

Dreams again have been shot down
Uncertainty brings deep frown
The seeds of love fully sown
Or a tear in wedding gown

They patched it up or so it seems
He - Oliver to reclaim gleam
She – Camrose to regain esteem
Canasta with Archie/Millie

Separation was perhaps too short
They didn't take time to again court
They chose to start anew not abort
The new honeymoon was way too short

Could not return to farm again
Unpleasant thoughts affected brain
He - to the field to plant some grain
She – inherited house in Wain

Together at night – just two
Her – wife, him – husband, like glue
As travel bug they pursued
At last wedded bliss ensued

Wayne Pendleton

Came strokes slowing her down
He tried to cope - no frown
To farm had to leave town
She had to cope on own

She'd lost many skills
Pondered he in hills
Must help her day fill
Know I can and will

It will be thus
I'll care and fuss
Not curse and cuss
Not me but us

Then the scare
Meant my care
Wouldn't wear
Now Health Care

Two years
All tears
Then fears
Not here

More
Tears
She's
Gone

## In Memoriam

*In memory of my beloved mother, who passed away at the age of ninety years plus one day on 19 May, 2007.*

# My Friend, Shorty

An excerpt from the soon-to-be-published autobiography of Wayne Pendleton entitled
*The Aussie with a Funny Accent*

He seemed like my enemy at first! Every day for a few months I'd arrive home from school with the inside of my thighs chafed from my new blue jean overalls riding up and down my legs as he walked, trotted, or galloped. The speed of movement didn't seem to make much difference to the chafing! Shorty was my means of transport, a black horse with white markings on his forehead and a couple of his ankle 'stockings'.

The chafing was bearable compared to the boils that developed from my bouncing up and down all the way to school and back, four miles each way, five days a week, ten months per year for four years. I'm not sure how long the boils lasted. It felt like forever, but it was probably only six to eight months, the bulk of Grade 3 at Batt School.

Shorty might have got his name because he was well short of being a thoroughbred. He was well short of speed anyway, especially when compared to Cousin Todd's Nicki who won every race amongst the cousins and their horses. Shorty always came last, probably more to do with his master's lack of riding skills than his shortage of speed. The most accurate description of Shorty that I can give is 'faithful plodder'. He plodded through the two-foot high snowdrifts in winter months, the mud and slush of spring, and the loose gravel in the drier summer months.

He didn't always make it through the snowdrifts, however. We were about one third of the way to school one morning when Shorty got bogged in a deeper than normal snowdrift that had hardened to the point that he could walk on the top of the drift without breaking through. That is what I thought, anyway. Sadly, I was wrong! Poor Shorty broke through the wind beaten toughened crust into the soft under layers of snow. He couldn't move! I couldn't move him. His belly rested on the tough crust that had not been broken by his hooves, about three feet (approximately one metre) above the road surface. He was high centred.

How was I going to get him out and back moving on the solid road surface? Uncle Alwyn who accompanied me to school where he was four grades above me in the one teacher school, must have become frustrated with the slow movement of Shorty and I and had ridden on ahead. He definitely wasn't there to help me in my dilemma anyway.

Shorty and I had not yet reached the road juncture where Margaret Miles and the Armitages normally joined us for the second half of our daily trip. Therefore I was left with no choice but to solve the problem myself. My moccasin covered feet were ineffective as mallets to break up the wind hardened crust, but as the bottom end of a lever comprised of my leg, I was able to gradually pry up small chunks of the crust from Shorty's legs forward. Then my mitten covered hands took on the major role of a shovel to slowly but surely open up two narrow paths.

I stomped, kicked, lifted, scooped, and carried compacted snow until I had freed Shorty's short legs (Ah! That's why his name is Shorty!); thus beating a ten metre path out of the snow bank onto the shallow snow covered section of the country road. I finally got to the tee intersection and turned right (East) for the final two miles to the school along the correction line road. There was no sign of any of the neighbour students, so the rest of the journey was just Shorty and me on our lonesome.

Quite the one-off experience it was, but there were other one-offs for Shorty and me. The most memorable had another winter setting. It was during a bitterly cold mid-winter period, probably January or February, generally the two coldest months in east-central Alberta in the 1940s. On almost every school day morning we checked the thermometer to gauge what extra scarves, muffs, and/or mitts might be needed to stave off the cold. The family must have had a bit of a sleep-in this particular morning because the thermometer check missed out as I was rushed out of the house by my mother and proceeded to put the bridle on Shorty, jumped on to his bare back, and left the barn and the farmyard at a gallop (Shorty, not me!)

Three miles into the four mile trip I was 'frozen' with

icicles hanging off my scarfed chin and frost forming on my eyebrows. Even my double-socked feet inside moccasins were in danger of frostbite, so I stopped at the only farm house along that section of the road. Mrs Meakins opened the door and in an astonished gasp cried out:"What are you doing here Wayne? There's no school today! It's 55 below!"

(Footnote for the uninformed: the temperature stated here is measured in Fahrenheit. I'm not sure of the exact conversion to Celsius (centigrade) but it approximates 50 degrees since minus 40 is the same in both measurements. In colloquial Australian lingo, we'd call that bloody cold!)

So I spent an hour or two warming nose and toes over the hot air grate, while I sipped on hot cocoa; then I made my way back home on my faithful plodder over the same roads but avoiding the fateful snowdrift in which we were previously trapped. Mrs Meakins must have got through to Mom on the party line telephone, because she sheepishly welcomed me home in a very apologetic way.

Shorty and I had a couple of other memorable adventures which I plan to relate, the first being an after school trip to the farm home of two brothers who also attended Batt school, Jim and Bill Lingley. Jim was a few years older than me and Bill was a couple of years younger. This visit wouldn't have been a problem if I had told my parents that I planned to stop there on the way home from school. Mind you such a stopover lengthened the journey by about two miles.

The problem was I hadn't told them had I? No such plans were even in my head when I left home that morning, but when the boys' parents asked if Helen (Mom) or Gordon knew I was planning to stay overnight, I said yes! I have never been a very convincing liar, so I am not sure whether they believed me or not. The party lines were out of action at the time so they couldn't confirm my stated parental approval. Anyway, I made no moves to go home, so the visit became a sleepover, much to my pleasure. However, this clandestine sleepover did not last all night, did it!

About midnight, I was awakened by a very angry stepfather Gordon, who harassed me briefly but crossly about the dreadful worry I had caused my mother by my disappearance. Gordon was pretty quiet on the way home, but he and his much-prized horse, Dummy virtually drove Shorty and I home like we were two calves that had strayed into a neighbour's field of oats.

I don't remember the matter being raised again, but I do remember that I never organised an impromptu sleepover at the Lingleys or anywhere else, that I can recall! My indiscretion seemed to cool the relationship between the two families as well and our occasional get-togethers seemed to end forever. I suppose Mom and Gordon were pretty cross at Buster and Lillian Lingley for letting me stay on into the night.

One event that occurred at that visit which might be of interest to readers involved the 'BB guns' that we children played with. For those that are unsure what a BB gun is, it is an air rifle that shoots tiny round balls called pellets, more a toy than a rifle that is intended to kill. After lining up a few empty tins and paper targets to practice on; Jim, Bill and I took turns with the one air rifle available aiming at each other's backsides. Against my loose fitting overalls the pellets tended to drop to the ground off the loose folds of the pant legs without even stinging. The Lingley brothers thought this not quite good enough, so they convinced me to bend over so that the denim cloth in the overalls would draw taut across my bottom. The effect was immediate and it was all I could do to keep from crying. This time the BB pellet had stung, but not nearly as much as the belt did when I received my just punishment at home later that night!

Wayne Pendleton

www.ingramcontent.com/pod-product-compliance
Lightning Source LLC
Chambersburg PA
CBHW051705090426
42736CB00013B/2543